I WONDER Why

There's a Hole In The Sky

and other questions about the environment

Sean Callery

KINGFISHER
NEW YORK

Published in the United States by Kingfisher,
175 Fifth Ave., New York, NY 10010
Kingfisher is an imprint of Macmillan Children's Books,
London.

Distributed in the U.S. and Canada by Macmillan,
175 Fifth Ave., New York, NY 10010

First published in 2008 by Kingfisher.

Consultant: Michael Chinery

Library of Congress Cataloging-in-Publication data has been
applied for.

ISBN: 978-0-7534-6799-2

Kingfisher books are available for special promotions and
premiums. For details contact: Special Markets Department,
Macmillan, 175 Fifth Ave., New York, NY 10010.

For more information, please visit www.kingfisherbooks.com

Printed in China
9 8 7 6 5 4 3 2 1
1TR/0612/UTD/WKT/140MA

Illustrations: Mark Bergin 25, 30–31; Martin Camm 18–19;
Peter Dennis (Linda Rogers Agency) 10, 12, 14–15, 26–27,
28; Chris Forsey cover, 16; Linden Artists 3, 9, 21, 22, 29;
Julian Baker title page, 6, 8, 10–11, 30–31; Peter Wilks (SGA)
all cartoons.

CONTENTS

4 Why is there life on Earth?

5 How can a star keep us warm?

5 What is the weather?

6 Which blanket keeps Earth warm?

7 How is the atmosphere like
a greenhouse?

7 What are greenhouse gases?

8 Why are trees the bee's knees?

8 How does water cycle?

9 Why can't we chop 'til we drop?

10 What makes gas?

10 Why is farming such a gas?

11 What's that smell?

12 Is it me or is it hot here?

12 Will this blow me away?

13 Has our climate always changed?

14 Are we up to our necks in floods?

15 What's wrong with car parks?

15 Who turned the rain off?

16 Why are poles hot stuff?

17 Why is ice so cool?

17 When is a river not a river?

18 Why is there a hole in the sky?

19 Is the hole there the entire time?

20 How can water be bad for you?

20 When is oil like glue?

21 Can air make you choke?

22 Why are some animals on the move?

22 Who needs a place to call home?

23 Who is a tiger's worst enemy?

24 What energy never runs out?

24 How can the Sun light up our nights?

25 How is wind farmed?

26 Why say 'bye to flying?

26 What are food miles?

27 Why all the fuss about taking a bus?

28 Why is garbage such a waste?

29 What are the three Rs?

29 When is a worm my friend?

30 How can I have a green house?

30 When is "off" not "off?"

31 Why are some lightbulbs greedy?

31 How else can I save energy?

32 Index

Why is there life on Earth?

There is life on Earth because it is not too hot and not too cold. We are just the right distance from the Sun, which gives us heat and light. This is why there is no life on our neighboring planets Venus (too hot) or Mars (too cold).

Sun

Mercury

Venus

Earth

Mars

Jupiter

Some experts call Earth "the Goldilocks planet" because, just like the porridge that Goldilocks eats in *Goldilocks and the Three Bears*, it is not too hot and not too cold.

How can a star keep us warm?

The Sun is a star, just like the ones we see in the sky at night. It looks bigger than the other stars because it is much closer to us. The Sun's rays are very hot and they warm Earth.

It takes about eight minutes for the Sun's rays to reach Earth across space. They travel the 93 million miles (150 million kilometers) at 1.1 million miles (1.8 billion kilometers) an hour.

Clouds are made of tiny drops of water. These bump into each other and make larger drops. When they get too big, they fall to the ground as rain or snow.

What is the weather?

There are all kinds of weather. It can be sunny, cloudy, wet, snowy, windy, or stormy. Both the Sun's heat and changes in the air above Earth affect the weather. The usual weather of a region or country is called its climate.

Some types of weather

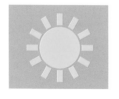

sunny

cloudy

heavy rain

thundery showers

snow

tropical storm

5

Which blanket keeps Earth warm?

Earth is surrounded by the atmosphere, which is made up of gases. It reaches a few hundred miles above the ground. The atmosphere has different layers (see right) and holds in heat like a blanket. It also helps protect us from the Sun's rays.

We can't see Earth's atmosphere because the gases in it are invisible. On Mars, the sky looks orangey-brown because its atmosphere is full of red dust.

Space

Exosphere

Thermosphere

Mesosphere

Stratosphere

Troposphere

How is the atmosphere like a greenhouse?

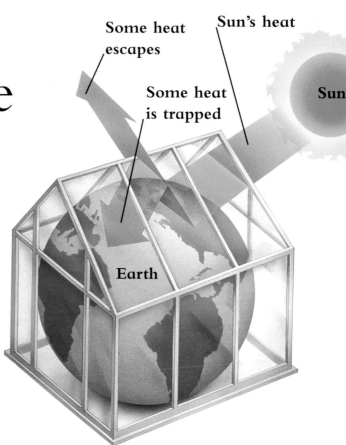

Some heat escapes

Sun's heat

Some heat is trapped

Sun

Earth

It gets very warm in a greenhouse as the glass walls and roof stop heat from escaping. Gases in our atmosphere trap heat in the same way and keep Earth warm. They are called greenhouse gases.

What are greenhouse gases?

The main greenhouse gas is water vapor (water that has turned into a gas). Other greenhouse gases include carbon dioxide, methane, and nitrous oxide (see pages 10–11). Some of these gases can remain in Earth's atmosphere for more than 100 years.

Greenhouse gases are made naturally and also by the things people do. For example, both volcanoes and cars blast out carbon dioxide.

Why are trees the bee's knees?

Trees take carbon dioxide from the air and they make oxygen, the gas we need to breathe. Trees also store carbon in their wood. If there were no trees, there would be so much carbon dioxide in the air that we wouldn't be able to breathe.

Rainforests are home to about two thirds of all the different types of animals and plants on Earth. In fact, thousands of them are found only in rainforests.

How does water cycle?

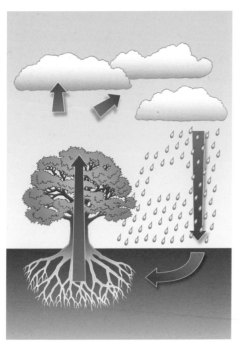

Water moves in a cycle. Tree roots soak up water. The water moves to the leaves and enters the air as vapor. This rises and turns into clouds. When it rains, the cycle starts again.

If you plant a tree, it will store carbon all of its life. This will help cut greenhouse gases.

Why can't we chop 'til we drop?

Cutting down and burning trees damages our planet. This is because there are fewer trees to make oxygen, and the ground left behind is likely to flood. Also, burning wood releases carbon dioxide into the atmosphere.

Over the last 60 years, about half of the world's rainforests have been cut down. This is so people can use the wood and the land.

9

What makes gas?

Carbon dioxide is given off by power stations burning coal, oil, and gas. A lot of carbon dioxide also comes from vehicles such as cars, trucks, and airplanes.

Those pretty, wispy trails that airplanes leave behind in the sky are not good for the planet. They are made from water vapor and exhaust fumes containing carbon dioxide.

Why is farming such a gas?

Some farmers put fertilizers that make nitrous oxide on their fields. Although there is not much of this gas in the atmosphere, it can hang around for 150 years. This is a problem because it traps heat.

What's that smell?

When cows break wind they release methane gas, which goes up into the atmosphere. Many animals (including us) produce methane. This gas also comes from rotting garbage and rice fields.

Rice farmer

Cows make a lot of methane because they eat so much grass. This makes gas when it goes through their digestive systems.

Is it me or is it hot here?

All around the world, temperatures are rising. This is global warming. In the summer of 2003, Europe was so hot that 35,000 people died, and there were forest fires. The summer of 2010 broke high-temperature records in many parts of the U.S.

The snow cap that has been at the top of Mount Kilimanjaro, in Africa, for 11,000 years is melting. Some scientists believe that within 20 years, the snow may have gone completely.

Will this blow me away?

The world is seeing more extreme weather, such as hurricanes, tornadoes, and typhoons. There are now twice as many big storms over the Atlantic Ocean as there were 100 years ago.

Has our climate always changed?

Earth has gone through several ice ages and different climates. For example, from 65 million years to 100 million years ago, the temperature was about 18°F (10°C) warmer, and dinosaurs lived in forests at the South Pole. But the climate has never changed as fast as it is changing at the moment.

Woolly mammoths lived in Siberia over 11,000 years ago. When temperatures rose by only a few degrees, it is possible that they couldn't stand the heat, and died out.

Are we up to our necks in floods?

The world seems to be suffering from more floods. Between 2005 and 2007, in Australia, the United States, India, the U.K., and eastern Europe, heavy rainfall caused landslides and made rivers burst their banks—flooding streets and houses. In 2010, one fifth of Pakistan's total land area was covered in floodwater after heavy monsoon rains, making millions of people homeless.

Scientists believe that five percent more rain, snow, and sleet is falling in the U.S. and Europe than 100 years ago.

What's wrong with car parks?

Building roads and car parks makes floods more likely because water is unable to soak into the ground. Instead, it runs quickly off the top of the hard surfaces, causing problems.

Lack of water is bad news, too. Australia suffered severe drought between 2001 and 2007, causing major water shortages. In 2011, eastern Africa faced the worst drought for 60 years—millions were affected by water and food shortages.

Who turned the rain off?

There have also been more droughts recently. In a drought, not enough rain falls. There is very little drinking water and it is difficult to grow crops. Since the 1970s, the number of serious droughts in the world has doubled.

Why are poles hot stuff?

The Earth spins around the North and the South poles. The North Pole is in the Arctic and the South Pole is in the Antarctic. Both poles are covered in ice, but rising temperatures are making it melt. Even a small rise in temperature can melt huge amounts of polar ice.

Soon there will not be enough sea ice in the Arctic for polar bears to live on. They are already losing weight as their hunting grounds disappear.

Why is ice so cool?

As ice is white, it reflects the Sun's rays and helps keep Earth cool. Ice caps are an important habitat (home) for animals such as polar bears and penguins.

If the entire Greenland ice sheet melted in the Arctic, sea levels would rise by 23 feet (7 meters). Countless coastal cities would be underwater and entire low-lying countries, such as Bangladesh, would be destroyed.

When is a river not a river?

The total surface area of the world's glaciers has shrunk by half in the last 100 years.

Glaciers are rivers of ice that move very slowly. They drain into streams which supply water to people farther down the river. Some glaciers are melting and getting smaller, so less water is reaching people.

Why is there a hole in the sky?

High up in the atmosphere is the ozone layer. It filters out the Sun's harmful rays. The ozone layer is damaged by chemicals called chlorofluorocarbons (CFCs for short), which were used in spray cans and fridges. CFCs have made a big hole in the ozone layer over Antarctica.

Hole in the ozone layer

Antarctica

18

Is the hole there the entire time?

No, the hole opens and closes with the seasons. The biggest hole so far was over Antartica in 2006. There is no hole above the Arctic, but the ozone has become thinner. CFCs have been used less since 1987, and the damage to the ozone layer has slowed.

CFCs have been replaced by hydrochlorofluorocarbons (or HCFCs) that are much less damaging, but even trickier to spell!

How can water be bad for you?

We need freshwater to live, but when chemicals and human waste get into rivers and lakes, water becomes polluted (dirty). This kills around five million people a year—that's around 14,000 deaths a day, just from dirty water.

When is oil like glue?

When oil tankers leak, it causes huge damage to the environment, especially to seabirds, seals, and sea otters. The oil sticks to their feathers or skin, and makes it hard for them to move or stay warm.

In April 2010, an oil-drilling rig in the Gulf of Mexico exploded, causing the worst environmental disaster in U.S. history. Many thousands of birds, fish, and sea creatures were killed.

Can air make you choke?

Smoke from factories and fumes from engine exhaust pipes send dirt and gas into the air, making it hard to breathe. In some cities, you can see the pollution hanging in the air. This is called smog.

In 1952, smog over London, U.K., killed 12,000 people. The dense fog was called a "pea souper" because it was thick, like pea soup.

Why are some animals on the move?

Animals sense when the climate changes and, as a result, some are moving to cooler regions. In North America, the red fox is moving into the Arctic and threatening the Arctic fox, which cannot compete with its bigger cousin.

Who needs a place to call home?

Elephants roam the grasslands of Africa and Asia. Much of this land is being turned into farmland, so the elephants are losing their habitat. This means that elephants could become extinct (die out).

Who is a tiger's worst enemy?

For a long time, people have hunted tigers for their skins and for their body parts, which are then used in medicines. Hunting tigers is now against the law in most countries, but some people still kill them illegally.

Many American pikas, or rock rabbits, are moving to higher land because they like cool temperatures. The warmer climate may make them extinct.

The dodo was a flightless bird that lived in Mauritius. It became extinct over 300 years ago when it was hunted to death.

What energy never runs out?

Energy from water, the wind, or the Sun is called renewable energy. Unlike oil, gas, or coal, it will never run out. Also, it does not produce carbon dioxide, so it will not speed up global warming.

Scientists are developing technology that extracts clean, reliable energy from the movement of waves. In the future, our homes could run on wave power.

How can the Sun light up our nights?

Solar cells use the Sun's rays to make electricity. They can be used for lights in the garden, or in roof panels to power whole houses. Solar collectors use the Sun's heat to warm water.

Solar panels

If we covered the Sahara Desert with solar panels, it would make more electricity than the world could use.

How is wind farmed?

People have used wind power for many years. The first wind-powered machines were windmills. Now, long blades spin at giant wind farms around the world. This type of farm can be built out at sea, too.

Some power stations burn plant material such as straw, willow, and elephant grass to make electricity.

Why say 'bye to flying?

Airplanes give off a huge amount of carbon dioxide. To travel in a "greener" way, take vacations closer to home instead of flying. If you have to fly, try to get a direct flight because taking off and landing use the most energy.

What are food miles?

If something you eat comes from another country, it traveled many "food miles" to get to you, and lots of carbon dioxide was produced on the way. Buying food grown locally is often better for the environment.

Why all the fuss about taking a bus?

Traveling by bus or train does less damage to the environment than going by car, because many people share the energy used.

Cycling and walking are much better for the environment than using a car because they do not burn oil.

If people share a car, they use less energy. Some roads have carpool lanes for cars carrying more than one person.

Why is garbage such a waste?

Most of our trash is burned, or buried in massive garbage dumps called landfills. Rain can wash poisons from the garbage through the soil and pollute the water supply. Landfills also release nasty gases into the air.

What are the three Rs?

Reduce, Reuse and Recycle—we should reduce what we throw away, reuse things as much as possible, and when we don't need them any more, recycle rather than dump them. As much as 70 percent of our garbage could be recycled.

Recycling one aluminum can saves enough energy to run a television for three hours.

When is a worm my friend?

Compost is an excellent way to reduce waste and help the garden. Put old leaves, plants, fruit and vegetable peelings, eggshells, and newspaper in a special bin outside. Worms and insects will turn it into soil for the garden.

Cut-up newspaper is perfect in a compost bin because it soaks up moisture. Then, tiny animals will munch away and break it up.

29

How can I have a green house?

A "green" home might have solar panels, solar collectors, and a wind turbine on the roof (see pages 24–25). Insulation would be fitted to keep the heat in. Outside, rainwater would be collected in a tank, and kitchen waste put in a compost bin.

Turn down the heating by a few degrees to save energy and cut the heating bills. You won't even notice the difference.

When is "off" not "off?"

Appliances left on standby, rather than turned off, use between 10 and 60 percent of the power they use when they are on. Turn off your television and computer monitor when you're not using them.

It is estimated that appliances on standby use up eight percent of all British power consumption in the home.

Solar panels

Solar collectors

Compost bin

Conservatory traps heat

Why are some lightbulbs greedy?

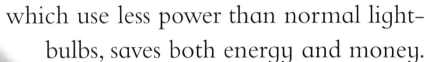

Most of the energy that goes into standard lightbulbs is changed into heat, not light. Switching to low-energy lightbulbs, which use less power than normal lightbulbs, saves both energy and money.

Wind turbine

Rainwater tank

Insulated walls

How else can I save energy?

Switch lights off when you can, and try not to use too much hot water. When you have a shower or bath, or make a hot drink, use only as much water as you need.

One energy-saving lightbulb uses up to 80 percent less electricity than an ordinary lightbulb yet it will last up to 12 times longer.

Index

A
airplanes 10, 26
Antarctica 18, 19
Arctic 16, 17, 19, 22
Arctic foxes 22
atmosphere 6, 7, 9, 10, 11, 18

C
carbon dioxide 7, 8, 9, 10, 24, 26
cars 7, 10, 15, 27
CFCs 18, 19
chemicals 18, 19, 20
climate 5, 13, 22, 23
clouds 5, 8
compost 29, 30
cows 11
cycling 27

D
dinosaurs 13
dodos 23
droughts 15

E
electricity 24–25, 31
elephants 22
energy 24–25, 26, 27, 29, 30–31

F
factories 21
farmers 10, 11
floods 9, 14, 15

food miles 26
forest fires 12

G
garbage 28–29
gases 6, 7, 8, 9, 10–11, 21, 24, 26, 28
glaciers 17
global warming 12, 24
greenhouse gases 7, 9

H
habitats 17, 22
hurricanes 12

I
ice 16, 17
ice ages 13
insulation 30, 31

L
landfills 28
lightbulbs 31

M
Mars 4, 6
methane 7, 11
Mount Kilimanjaro 12

N
nitrous oxide 7, 10
North Pole 16

O
oil 10, 20, 24, 27
oxygen 8, 9
ozone layer 18–19

P
penguins 17
pikas 23
polar bears 16, 17
poles 16–17
pollution 20–21
power stations 10, 25

R
rain 5, 8, 14, 15, 28, 30, 31
rainforests 8, 9
recycling 28–29
red foxes 22
roads 15, 27
rock rabbits see pikas

S
seabirds 20
seals 20
sea otters 20
smog 21
solar cells 24
solar collectors 24, 30
solar panels 24, 30
South Pole 13, 16
Sun 4, 5, 6, 7, 17, 18, 24

T
tigers 23
tornadoes 12
travel 26–27
trees 8–9
typhoons 12

V
Venus 4

W
water 5, 7, 8, 10, 14, 15, 17, 20, 24, 28, 30, 31
water cycle 8
wave power 24
weather 5, 12
wind 5, 24, 25, 30, 31
wind farms 25
windmills 25
wind turbines 25, 30, 31